Illustrations by Ang

PUBLISHED BY STUDIO PUBLICATIONS (IPSWICH) LIMITED
32 PRINCES STREET, IPSWICH, SUFFOLK, ENGLAND

Billy Blackberry is one of the Munch Bunch.

He lives in an old wooden box with his best friend Scruff Gooseberry.

He is usually naughty.

He doesn't even have to try.

He just is.

Billy Blackberry and Scruff Gooseberry were very untidy.

Their house was a mess.

But they didn't care.

They would rather play games or be naughty than clean their house.

Today, they were going to try not to be naughty.

They were going to play hide-and-seek instead.

While Scruff closed his eyes, Billy ran off to hide.

Scruff started to count, "1–2–3 . . .".

Billy hid behind Sally
Strawberry's easel.

He didn't think Scruff would find
him there.

He thought that if he couldn't see
Scruff, Scruff couldn't see him.

Silly Billy.

Billy could hear Scruff still counting.

". . . 98–99–100. I'm coming to find you," Scruff called.

Billy decided to hide somewhere different.

And as he ran away he stepped right onto a tube of Sally's paint.

Naughty Billy.

He ran off to hide behind Lizzie Leek's cooking-pot home.

"Scruff will never think of looking for me here," Billy thought.

But he didn't know that he had red paint on his shoes, did he?

Lizzie had just baked a pie.
A candy-floss and treacle pie.
Billy's favourite.

He could not resist the temptation.

He just had to have a piece.

So as soon as Lizzie had gone, he helped himself.

Just like that.

Very naughty Billy.

Then he heard Scruff coming.

So he ran to hide behind Pete Pepper's flower-pot house.

Pete Pepper saw the red footprints in his garden.

He decided to investigate.

Billy knew that Pete would be very angry if he caught him behind his house.

So as soon as Pete opened his door, Billy ran away.

DISASTER!

He trod right on Pete Pepper's new model aeroplane.

Now, Pete Pepper is usually a very angry pepper.

But this made him a very, very angry pepper.

He jumped up and down in anger.

Soon, Lizzie Leek, Sally Strawberry and Scruff Gooseberry arrived.

They had followed the red footprints.

Billy decided to hide in an old shopping-bag.

"Scruff will never find me here," he thought.

Billy made himself very comfortable.

He was still eating candy-floss and treacle pie when the others arrived.

"I wonder where he could be," said Scruff. "The footprints stop here."

Suddenly there was the sound of a loud RIP.

The old shopping-bag had split.

Billy fell right in front of the others.

"Found you!" yelled Scruff, very pleased with himself.

But the others weren't so pleased.

"First of all," said Lizzie, "you must wash away all the red footprints. Then you must help me make another pie."

"And get me some more red paint," said Sally.

"And help me make another model aeroplane," shouted Pete.

"Oh dear," said Billy. "And just because we played hide-and-seek."

A.M.

"It's a good job I didn't decide to be naughty today," he said to no one in particular.